Let's Learn About France

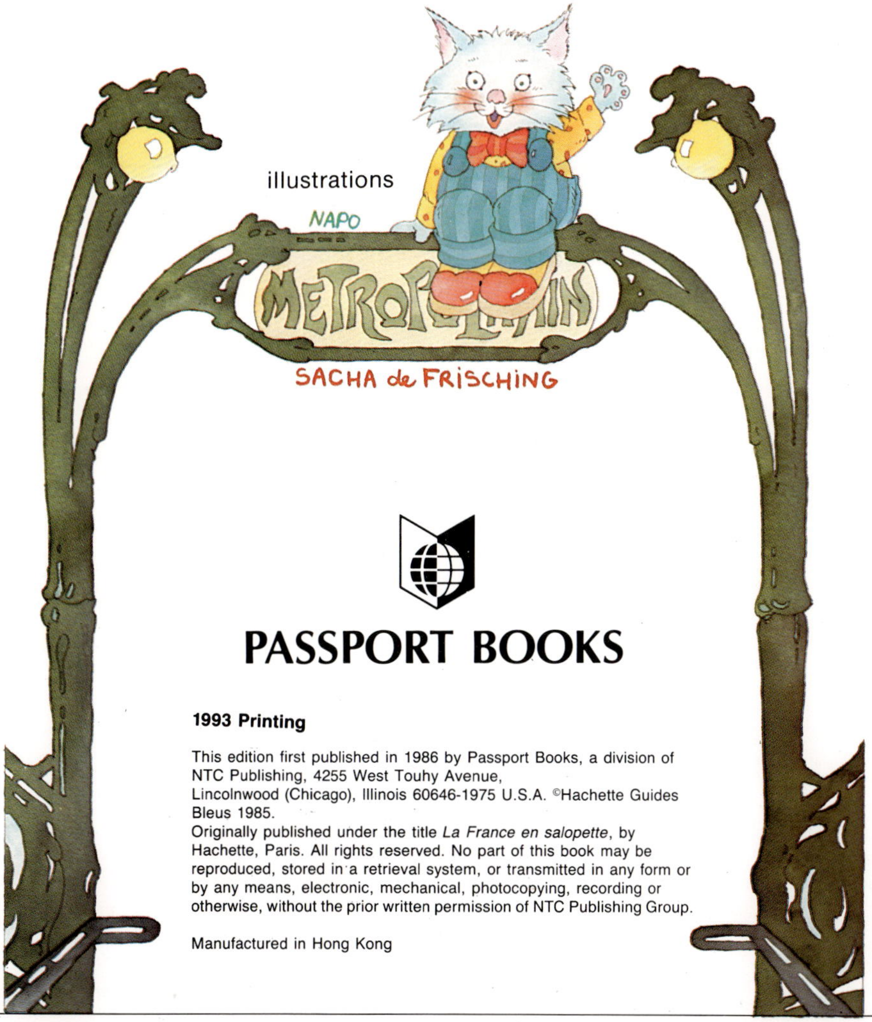

illustrations
NAPO

SACHA de FRISCHING

PASSPORT BOOKS

1993 Printing

This edition first published in 1986 by Passport Books, a division of NTC Publishing, 4255 West Touhy Avenue, Lincolnwood (Chicago), Illinois 60646-1975 U.S.A. ©Hachette Guides Bleus 1985.
Originally published under the title *La France en salopette*, by Hachette, Paris. All rights reserved. No part of this book may be reproduced, stored in a retrieval system, or transmitted in any form or by any means, electronic, mechanical, photocopying, recording or otherwise, without the prior written permission of NTC Publishing Group.

Manufactured in Hong Kong

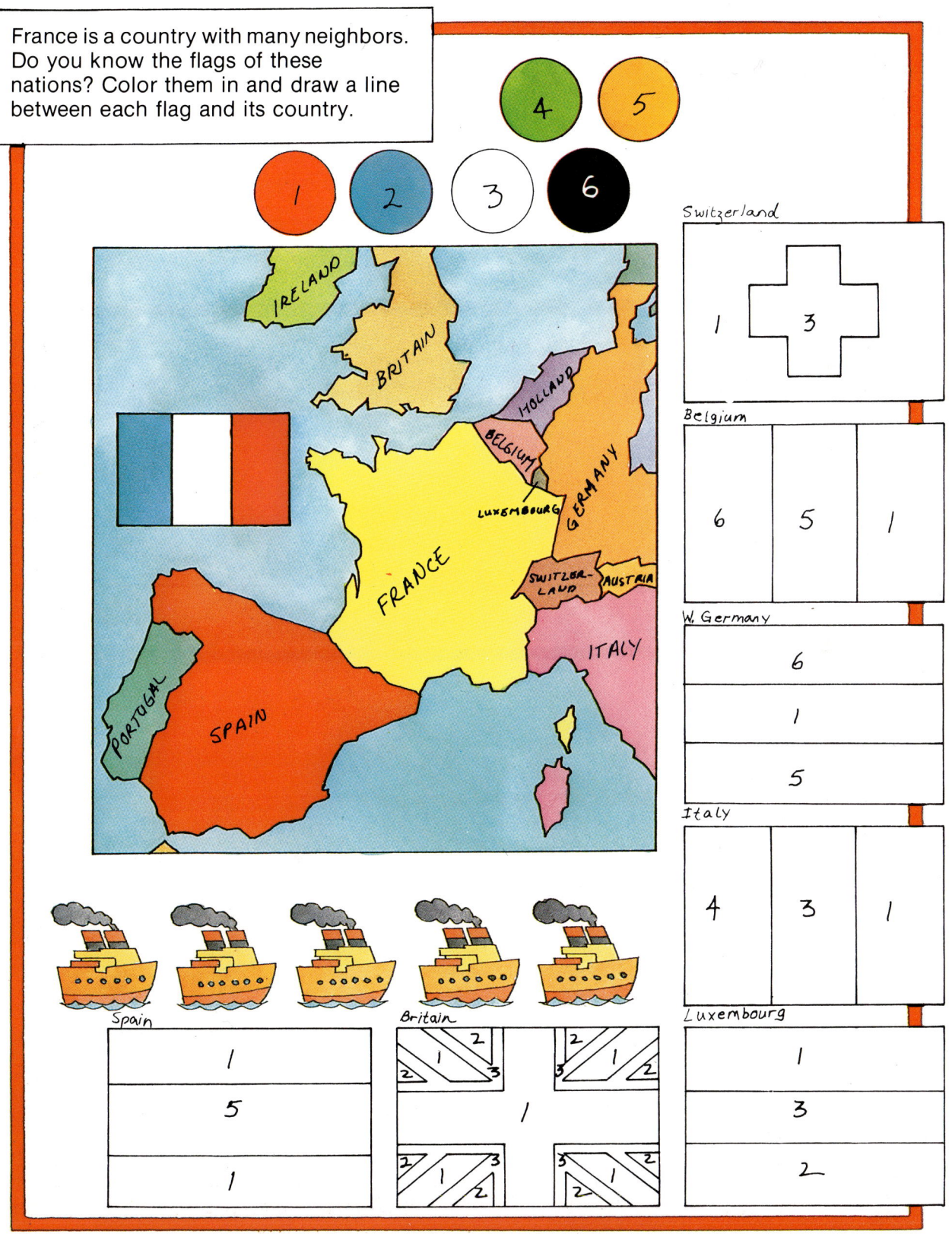

Bonjour les amis

This is a secret message.
To crack the code,
find the letters that match
the drawings.

Color anything that moves on wheels red,
anything that flies blue, anything that floats green,
and anything that glides yellow.

From coast to coast

France has a great variety of coasts. Many of them are named after a color. To get to know them, follow my instructions and color in the umbrellas with the matching color.

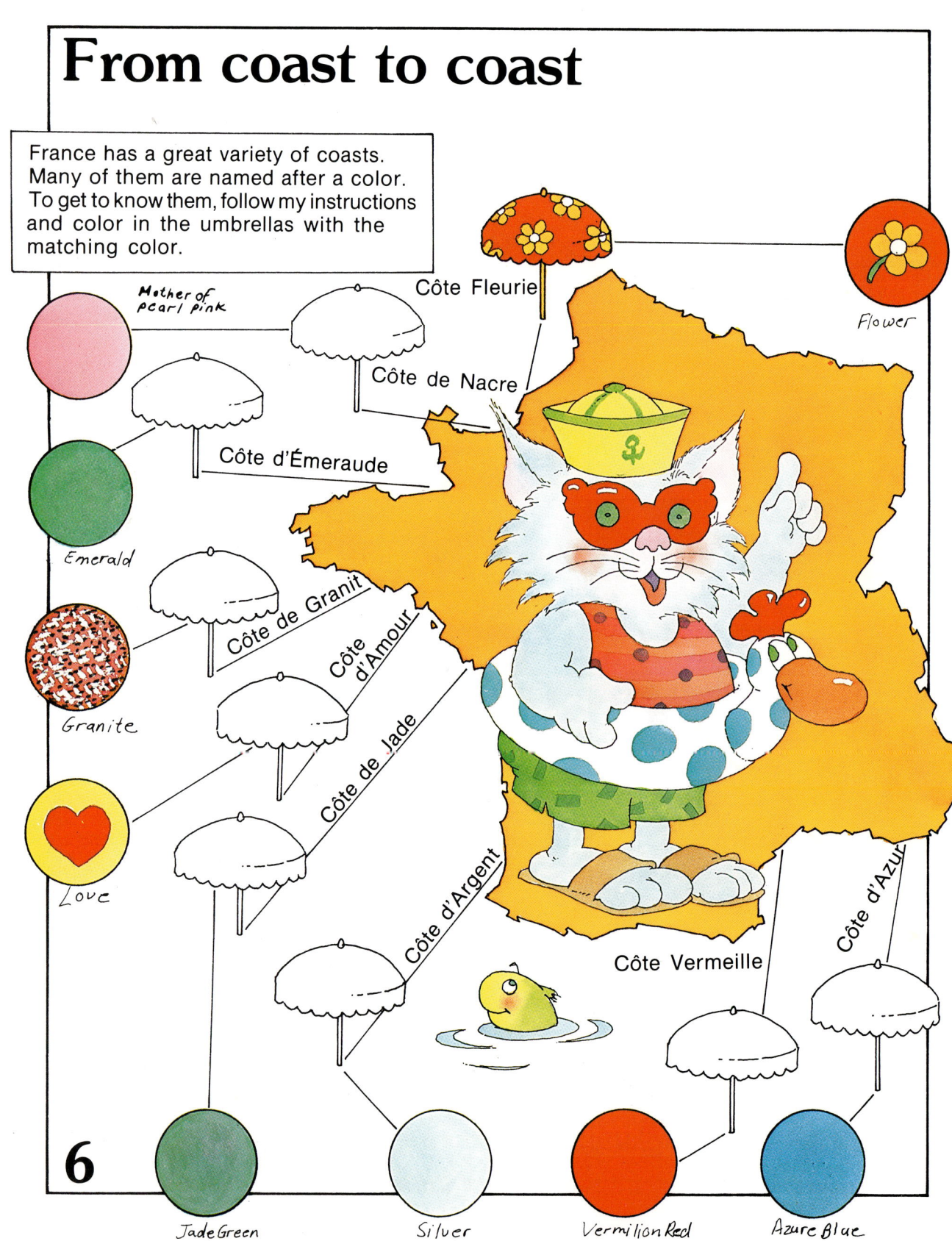

Mother of pearl pink
Emerald
Granite
Love
Jade Green
Silver
Vermilion Red
Azure Blue
Flower

Côte Fleurie
Côte de Nacre
Côte d'Émeraude
Côte de Granit
Côte d'Amour
Côte de Jade
Côte d'Argent
Côte Vermeille
Côte d'Azur

6

Trace a larger version of the square below on wet sand.
Then, decorate it as shown here with things found on the beach such as pebbles, shells and seaweed.

J'aime Paris

Discover Paris, the capital of France, as you play this board game. You'll need: a die, bottle tops to use as counters, and a bag of **berlingots** (candy) for the winner. The first player to throw a 6 starts the game.

You are feeling sick. Moan and groan!

To get a better view of the **Place de la Concorde** move back 7 squares.

Join the player who is ahead for a snapshot in front of the **Opéra**.

Bravo! **C'est gagné**. You've won.

You are picnicking at the **Trocadéro** and miss 2 turns.

Pretend to speak while licking some ice cream and throw the die again.

You are admiring Paris from **Sacré-Coeur**, on top of **Montmartre**.

You are taking a rest in the **Jardin du Luxembourg** and miss 2 turns.

You are in a hurry. Hop on the **Métro** and advance to number 9.

You greet Napoléon at the **Place Vendôme** and miss 1 turn.

14 You walk down the **Champs-Elysées** to number 19.

13 You are climbing the **Arc de Triomphe**. You miss 2 turns.

12 To advance to number 23, sing a song on this bridge over the Seine.

11 You are reading **Paris-Match** and miss 1 turn.

25 You can see the **Tour Eiffel**. Throw a 1 to finish.

24 Time for some window shopping. Go back to square 16.

23 At the **Invalides** you have to wait for an even number to move on.

10 You are watching a puppet show at the **Tuileries**. Back to 9.

20 You miss 2 turns to take a pony ride at the **Jardin d'Acclimatation**.

21 Au secours! Help! All the players come to your rescue.

22 Return to number 18 for lunch.

9 Like the bells of **Notre-Dame** cathedral count to 12 in French.

5 Take the **bateau-mouche** to **Notre-Dame** in square 9.

6 You are cycling through the **Bois de Boulogne**. Go back to number 1.

7 The Children's Workshop at the **Centre Pompidou**. Move to number 12.

8 Imitate an animal at the **Jardin des Plantes** and throw a 6 to move on.

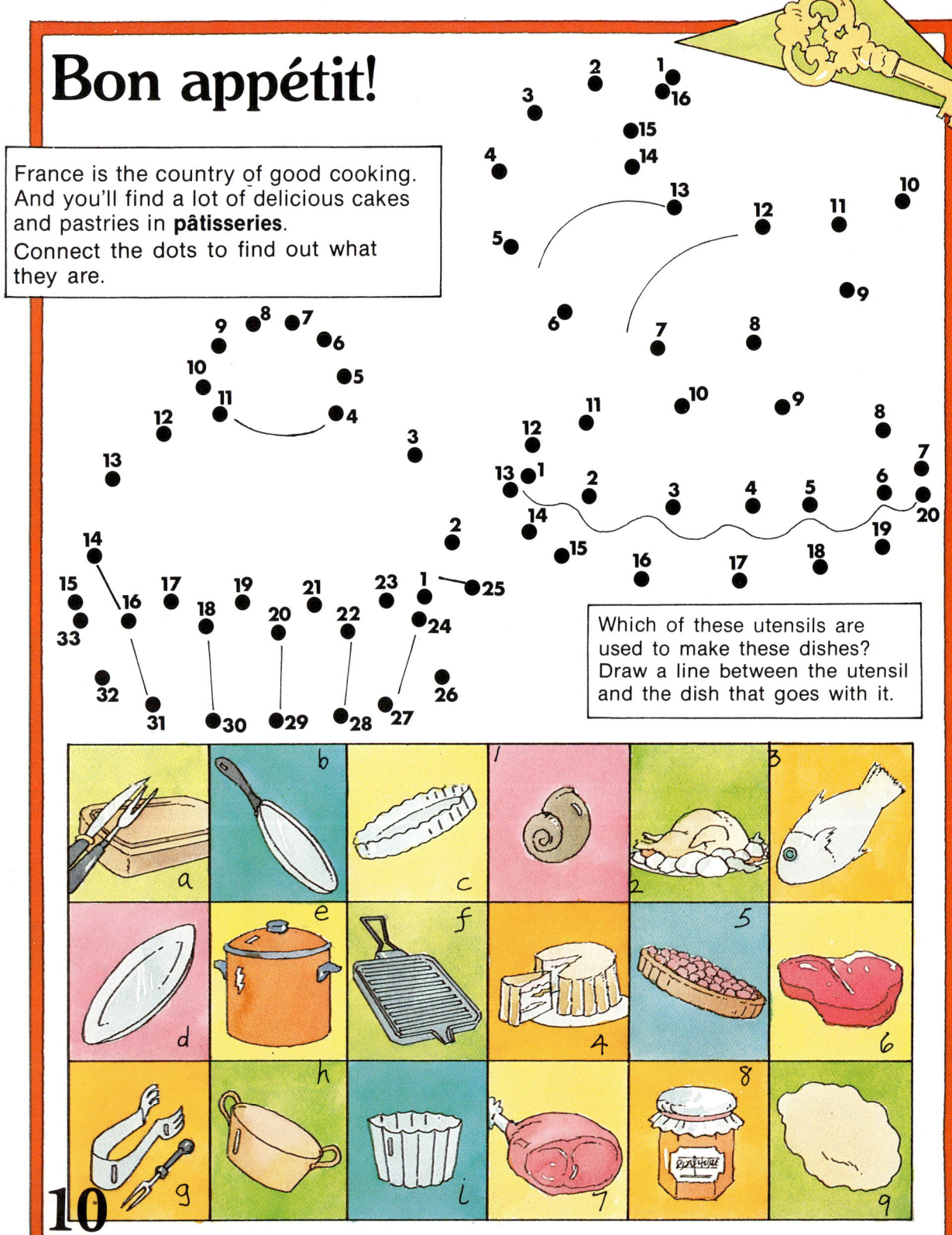

Become a real cordon bleu chef
and try out this recipe for **tomates niçoises**.

1 Cut a few slices of cucumber, then dice the rest. Leave to drain.

2 Wash and dry the tomatoes. Cut off the tops of the tomatoes and clean them out with a teaspoon. Turn them upside down and leave to drain.

3 In a bowl, mix oil, vinegar, mustard, salt and pepper. Then stir in the diced cucumber and a can of tuna.

4 Stuff the tomatoes with this mixture, arrange them on a plate and decorate them with the cucumber slices, the black olives and the parsley.

You'll need:

Tuna, Cucumber, Mustard, Olives, Oil, Vinegar, Salt, Pepper, Parsley, 4 Tomatoes

During the Revolution, men who wore pants with red, white and blue stripes were nicknamed **Sans-Culottes**.

For the **cocarde** (badge) on your hat, you'll need:

4 strips of red crêpe paper 2 in. x 10 in.
4 strips of white crêpe paper 2 in. x 8 in.
4 strips of blue crêpe paper 2 in. x 6 in.

How about making you own **Sans-Culotte** outfit?

You'll need:
pajama bottoms
red, white and blue ribbons
a blue vest
red, white and blue buttons
a red scarf

Sew or glue the ribbons on the pajamas. Put on a white shirt and tie a red scarf around your waist. Decorate the vest with the buttons.

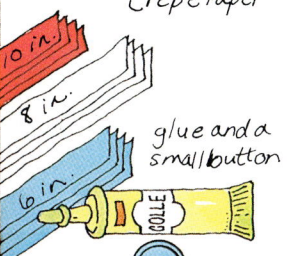

Look, I'm a Sans-Culotte!

Remember the place?

This is a game for 2.
The first player takes a good look at the pictures, then closes his (her) eyes while the other player covers 3 pictures with little white squares.
Then, the first player looks and tries to remember the hidden pictures while the other counts to 10.

Ready for a dance?

Sur le pont d'Avignon,
On y danse, on y danse,
Sur le pont d'Avignon,
On y danse tous en rond...

In the old days, each region had its own costumes.
You can still see them at festivals.
Which of these boys and girls are going to dance with each other?
Draw a line between the shapes and dancers that make a perfect match.

There are some musical instruments hidden in this drawing. Color in the ones you have found.

Frère Jacques, Frère Jacques
Dormez-vous, dormez-vous?
Sonnez les matines, sonnez les matines,
Dig, ding, dong, dig, ding, dong!

One, two, three — go!

The 24 hours of Le Mans
is a famous car race.
But who is going to win this race?

In the south of France, **le Midi**, almost everybody likes to play **pétanque**. Each player has two steel **boules** (balls), which he has to throw as closely as possible to a smaller ball, called the **cochonnet**.

If you want to try this game, here's how to make your own set of **boules**.

You'll need:
play dough
felt pens
varnish

Make 6 large round balls with your dough. Draw some lines on them with a pencil and leave to harden in a dry place. You can then paint them different colors.

To finish, cover with a coat of varnish.

Sports and games

Le football and **le rugby**
are very popular sports in France.
How many balls can you see on the field?

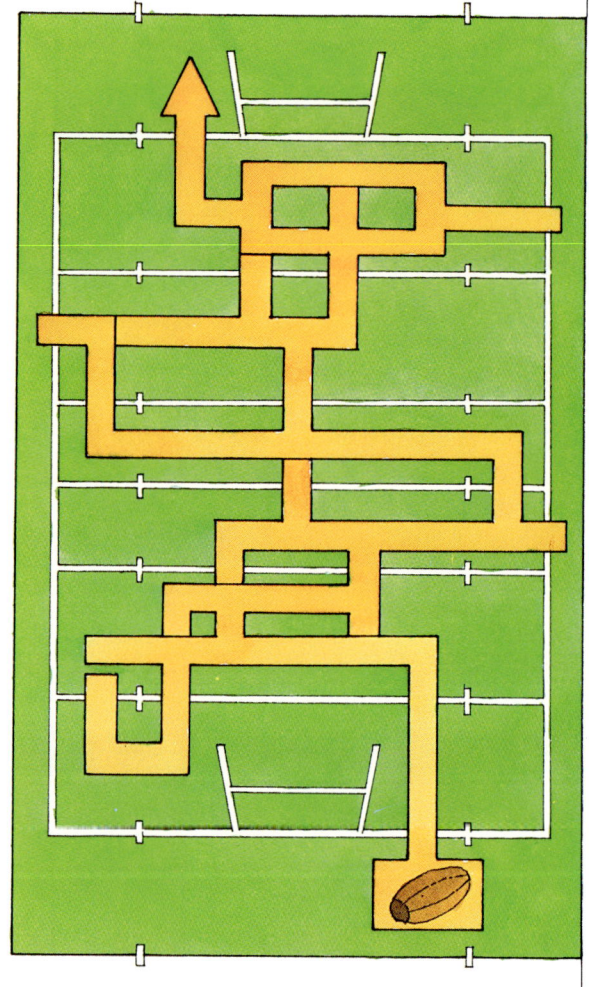

Here is a ball game to keep you in shape.

All players stand in a circle.
One of them throws or kicks the ball
up high and shouts another player's name.
Everybody has to run as far as possible
while the one who has been called
tries to catch the ball. As soon as
the player's got the ball, everybody has
to stop. He or she can now take 5 steps
and aim the ball at another player
who starts a new game when hit.

Cycling is another great French passion. The first **Tour de France** took place in 1903.

Give each bike back to the right cyclist.

Vive la France!

Here are 6 famous characters from French history. Using 3 colors only, try to color each of them in a different way.

LOUIS XIV
the Sun King

NAPOLÉON I
the emperor who wanted to conquer Europe

VERCINGÉTORIX
the chief of the Gauls

MARIE-ANTOINETTE
the queen who died on the guillotine

JEANNE D'ARC
who freed France from the English

SAINT-LOUIS
the very holy king

Bravo, j'ai gagné!
Hurray, I've won!

Mark all the things you know in French with an **X**.
You score 5 points as soon as you have **3 X's** in a row, either across or down, or even diagonally!

Your grand total:

Wrapping gifts

Into which of these boxes would you put the gifts you have bought for your friends?
Find the right box for each gift.

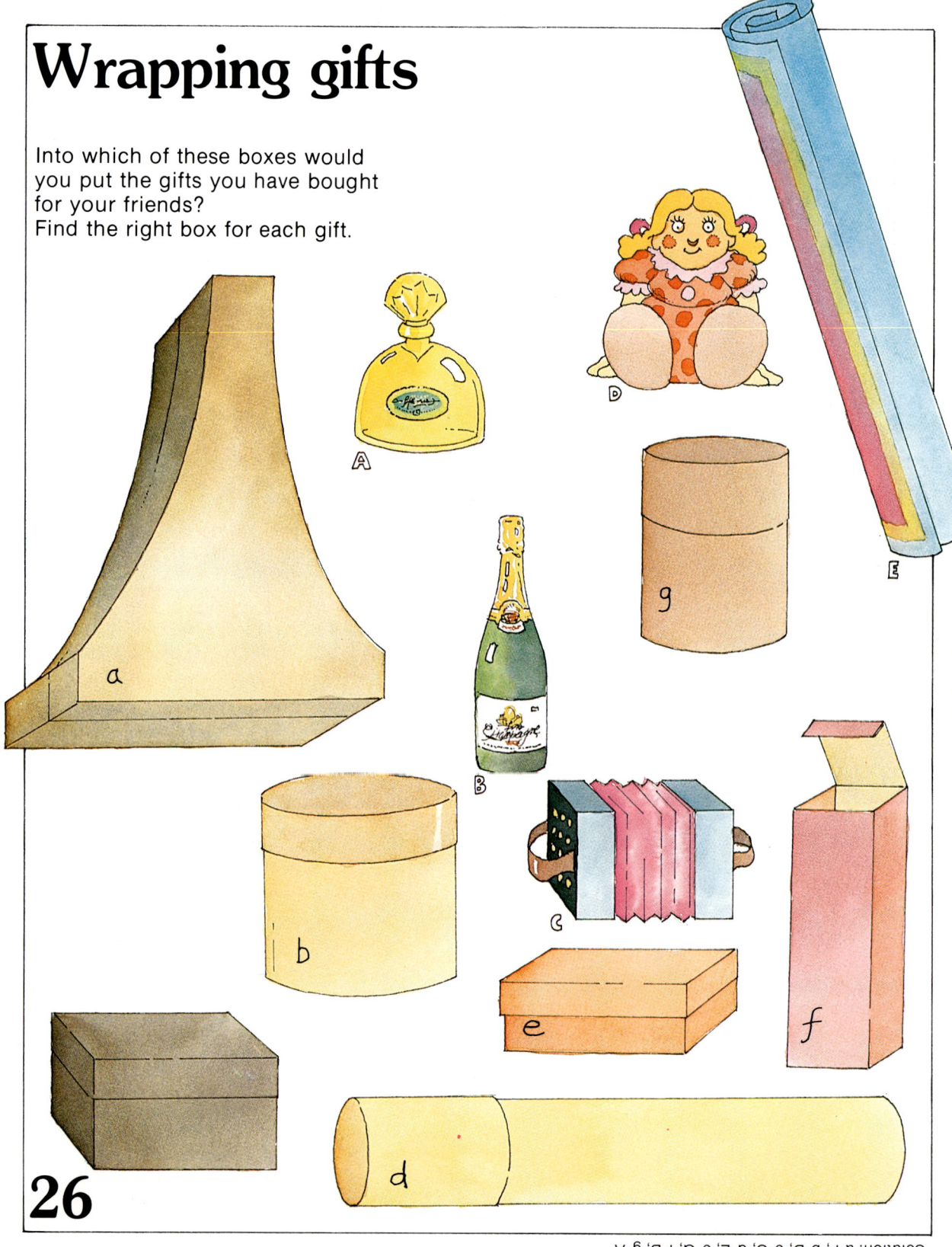

Solution: a-F, b-D, c-C, d-E, e-G, f-B, g-A

Bluebeard—A French Fairy Tale

Once upon a time there was a very rich man who was unlucky enough to have a blue beard. It made him look so terrible that everybody was afraid of him...

Now one of his neighbors had two daughters, one just as beautiful as the other. Bluebeard wished to marry one of them, but he was happy to leave the choice to their mother. Unfortunately neither girl wanted to marry Bluebeard because rumor had it that he had been married several times before and that all his wives had mysteriously disappeared...

So Bluebeard invited the two sisters and several of their girlfriends to his castle. And for eight days there were celebrations, dancing and laughter. Things went so well that the younger sister didn't find his beard quite so blue any more and was delighted to marry him.

After a month, Bluebeard had to go away on a trip. He entrusted his wife with the keys of the castle and encouraged her to invite all her friends during his absence.... But he made it quite clear that she was not to open the small room at the end of the corridor.

Full of wonder, her friends and neighbors arrived to discover the marvels of the castle. They envied their lucky friend. But she hardly took any notice of them because she had only one thing on her mind: to explore the forbidden room.

Finally she could resist the temptation no longer and, with trembling hands, she opened the door. What she

saw filled her with horror. All Bluebeard's former wives were lying there, with their throats cut. She thought she was going to die of fright and, in her shock, dropped the key on the blood-stained floor. No matter how much she scrubbed the key, the stains just wouldn't go away. . . .

Bluebeard, on his return, knew immediately what had happened and shouted: 'You wanted to see inside the room, so now it's your turn to go in there!' The poor woman threw herself at his feet and begged him, in tears. But it was no good. Bluebeard had a heart of stone; he only let her have a few moments to pray before she died.

She called to her sister: 'Anne, my sister Anne, can't you see anybody coming? Our brothers promised to come today!'

'I can see nothing but the sun blazing and the cows grazing,' Anne replied staring at the horizon. Then Bluebeard howled and waved his great knife and the entire castle trembled.

'Anne, my sister Anne, can't you see anything?'

'Nothing but the sun blazing and the cows grazing. . .'

'Enough of this, you will have to die,' Bluebeard shouted, raising his huge knife.

But at that very moment there was a knock on the door and in came two knights. Their brothers had arrived in time! They threw themselves on Bluebeard and killed him, and so they put an end to his reign of terror. And they all lived happily ever after.

Logbook

Before each flight, the pilot fills in his logbook.
Here is one for you to complete for the trip of your dreams.

Date:
Flight number:
Airport of departure:
Altitude:
Destination:
Speed:
Weather conditions:
Stopover at:
Arrival time:
Departure time:
Route:
Fuel:
Crew:
Type of aircraft:
Cargo weight:
Number of passengers:
Name of copilot:
Name of pilot:

Au revoir...

Did you notice the little pictures hidden throughout the book? Each of them goes with one of these pictures. Can you match them up?

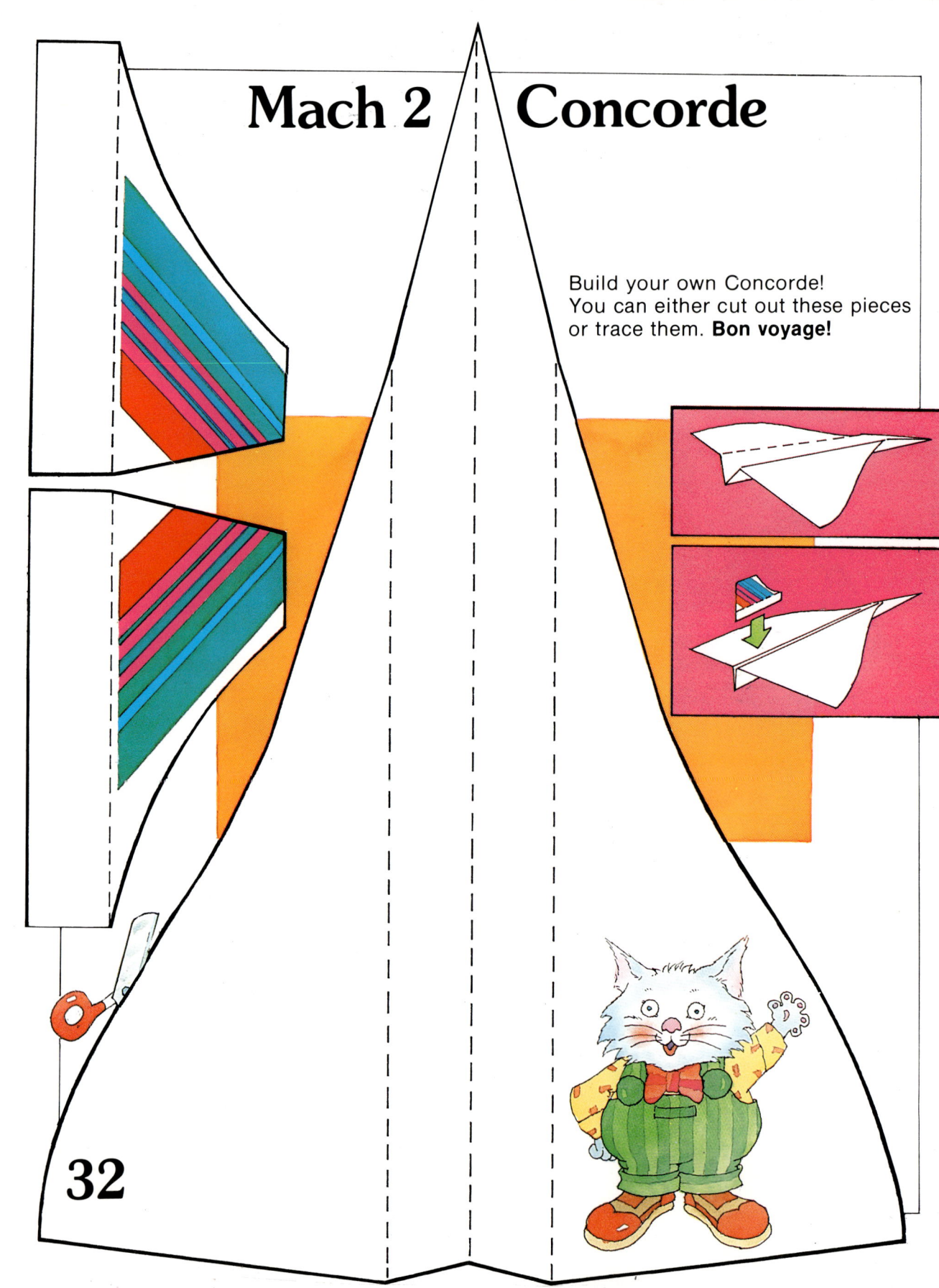